A New True Book

JUNGLES

By Illa Podendorf

*This "true book" was prepared
under the direction of
Illa Podendorf,
formerly with the Laboratory School,
University of Chicago*

CHILDRENS PRESS, CHICAGO

Bamboo trees in a jungle

PHOTO CREDITS

James P. Rowan—2, 12, 15, 23, 25 (bottom), 29, 30 (right), 32 (2 photos), 33 (2 photos), 34, 35 (2 photos), 36 (2 photos), 37 (2 photos), 38 (left), 45 (bottom left).

Lynn M. Stone—4, 9 (left), 21, 45 (right).

A. Kerstitch—6, 9 (top), 18 (2 photos), 25 (top), 26, 28 (right), 40 (bottom), 45 (top left).

Mark Rosenthal—9 (right), 14, 16, 27, 31, 38 (right), 40 (top).

Len Meents—10.

Allan Roberts—Cover, 28 (left).

Candee & Associates—30 (left).

Colour Library International—42, 43.

Cover: Parrots

Library of Congress Cataloging in Publication Data

Podendorf, Illa.
  Jungles.

  (A New true book)
  Previously published as: The true book of jungles. 1959.
  Includes index.
  Summary: Discusses the climate and locations of jungles and describes the plants of which jungles are made and the animals and people that live in jungles.
    1.   Jungle ecology—Juvenile literature.
[1.   Jungles] I. Title.
QH541.5.J8P63 1982   574.5′2642   82-4454
ISBN 0-516-01631-8   AACR2

TABLE OF CONTENTS

WHAT ARE JUNGLES?

A jungle has many kinds of plants. They grow close together.

It is always warm, damp, and dark in a jungle! The heat and rain help the plants to grow quickly. Sometimes a jungle is called a tropical "rain forest."

Jungles of Yucatán Peninsula

In a jungle, tall trees reach for the sun. Shorter trees branch out beneath them. Ferns and bushes cover the ground. Vines climb everywhere. They seem to tie the plants together.

Sometimes the edge of a jungle looks like a green wall. It is thick with plants.

The roof of a jungle is made of the tops of tall trees held together with vines. It is bright with flowers and fruit. Sometimes it is called "high jungle."

Many plants make good food for animals. There are many animals in a jungle where there is good food.

Top: Tropical butterfly
Above: Bengal tiger
Right: Toucan

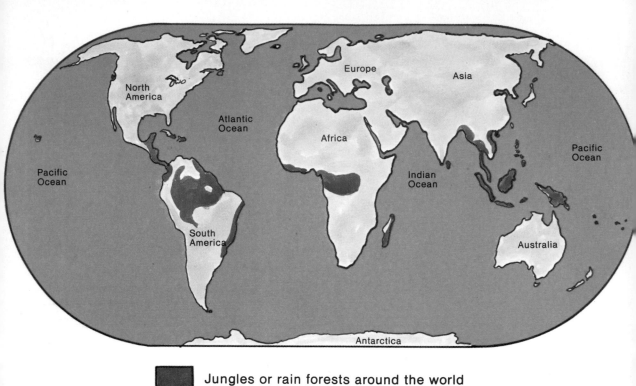

Jungles or rain forests around the world

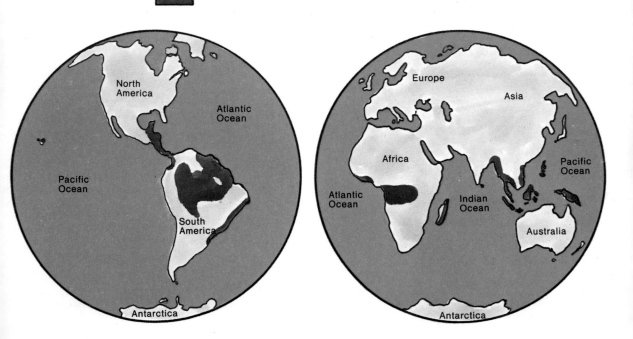

WHERE ARE JUNGLES?

Jungles grow only in the warmest parts of the earth. These places are near the equator.

At the equator the sun shines directly on the earth. The weather here is almost the same, summer and winter. It is always warm. Rain falls almost every day.

There are jungles in South and Central America, Africa, and Asia.

There are islands in the Pacific Ocean that are almost all jungles.

WHAT KINDS OF PLANTS MAKE A JUNGLE?

Many kinds of trees grow in a jungle. Most of them grow tall and straight. Most of their leaves and flowers are near the top in the sunshine.

Small trees spread and branch under the taller trees. They get less sunlight than the taller trees.

Some trees have very slender trunks that spread wide near the ground.

Strangler fig

Many strangler trees
grow in jungles. These
plants have roots that grow
around the plants they live
on and strangle them.

There are many kinds of
vines in a jungle.

Some vines have stems as thin as string. Some vines have stems as big around as your arm.

Vines grow very long. They climb to the top of tall trees.

Orchids grow in jungles. They usually grow far above the ground, fastened to other plants.

Jungle orchids

Orchids are air plants.
Air plants get their food
from water and air.

Ferns and palms grow
close to the ground in a
jungle.

Some ground plants
have leaves of gold or red
or white.

Certain kinds of mushrooms grow in a jungle among the ferns and palms.

Bamboo is a kind of grass that grows in a jungle. It grows as tall as a tree. It may grow as tall as a four-story building. It grows very fast. It may grow sixteen inches in one day.

Bamboo

Some house plants are relatives of plants of a jungle. A periwinkle grows close to the ground in our gardens. It is a tree in jungles.

Jungle plants are losing leaves and getting new ones all the time. It is never so dry or cold that they stop growing. The jungle is always green.

WHAT KINDS OF ANIMALS LIVE IN A JUNGLE?

A jungle is a home for many kinds of animals. Some of them live on the ground.

Agouti

Some live among the plants, part way up.

Some live in the roof of the jungle.

Many kinds of insects live in a jungle. Some of them are hard to see. They look like what they live upon.

Laternfly beetle

Goliath beetle

Birdwing butterfly

Many kinds of ants live in the jungle. Butterflies, cockroaches, beetles, spiders, and crickets live there, too.

Some birds of the jungle eat the insects.

Many birds live among the bright flowers and fruits at the roof of the jungle.

The jungle turkey, a curassow, lives in cocoa trees that grow in jungles.

Great curassow

Giant green frogs live in the jungle trees.

Gecko lizards and iguana lizards live in jungles, too.

Gecko lizard

Iguana

Boa constrictors (left) are
not poisonous snakes.
Cobras (above) are poisonous
snakes.

   Many different kinds of
snakes live in a jungle.
Most snakes live on the
ground. Sorne live in trees.

Armadillos curl into a ball to protect
themselves from their enemies.

The armadillo lives on
the ground in a jungle. It
has a special claw on its
front feet. This claw helps
it to dig into nests of ants
and termites.

Giant anteater

Giant anteaters live on the ground where ants are found easily.

The tamandua, or lesser anteater, can hang in the trees by its long tail. It eats ants, too.

The silky anteater travels at night to look for ants.

Tapir

Black jaguar

The tapir and jaguar are jungle animals. The jaguar is a cousin of the tiger. It is an enemy of the tapir.

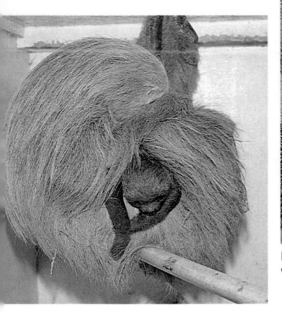

Hoffman's sloth (above), a mother sloth with her baby (left)

A sloth is an upside-down animal. It hangs head down from a tree branch. It looks like a ball of hanging moss. A sloth moves slowly.

Collared peccary

A wild pig, the peccary, lives in jungles. These pigs have small tusks but they are as sharp as razors. They run in packs, and roam the jungles at night.

No one wants to meet a pack of these wild pigs.

Many monkeys live in jungles.

Some kinds of monkeys live only in jungles in South America or Central America.

White-eared marmoset (above) and owl monkey (left)

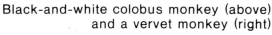
Black-and-white colobus monkey (above)
and a vervet monkey (right)

Other kinds of monkeys
live only in jungles of the
other parts of the world.

Capybara (above) and an arrow
poison frog (left)

Here are some of the
animals that live in a
South or Central American
jungle.

Potto (above) and rhino hornbill (right)

These animals live in jungles of other parts of the world.

Some kinds of animals live in jungles everywhere.

DO PEOPLE
LIVE IN JUNGLES?

Some jungles have almost no people living in them.

Other jungles have a few people living in them.

There are a few jungles where many people live.

Jungle homes in Africa (above) and Mexico (below)

Most people of the
jungles get their homes,
food, and clothing from the
jungle.

Jungle people are not all
alike. They do not speak
the same language. They
do not act and look alike.

Some are warlike.

Some are peaceful.

Some raise plants and
animals for food. Others
eat wild plants and
animals.

Many children of the
jungle go to school. But
they learn many things
from their parents, too.

Children on
the Fiji Islands

African
children

They learn which plants are good to eat. They learn which plants will help the sick.

They learn how to hunt animals and to know their tracks when they see them.

WHAT GOOD ARE JUNGLES?

We get spices, medicines, oils, chocolate, nuts, balsa wood, rubber, bamboo, and many other things from the jungles.

Scientists go to jungles to study the plants, animals, and people that live there.

Orchids (top left),
Candlebush (left),
Macaw (above)

We are learning to make
more uses of the jungles
all the time, as we marvel
at the wonder and the
beauty of them.

WORDS YOU SHOULD KNOW

Africa(AFF • rih • ka) —one of the seven continents.

Asia(A • ja) —a continent east of the continent of Europe.

armadillo(arm • ah • DILL • oh) —an animal with a bony body covering that digs into the ground.

balsa(BALL • sa) —a tree that grows in warm places that has light, strong wood.

bamboo(bam • BOO) —a tall grass that looks like a tree. It grows in warm places.

claw —a sharp, curved nail on the toe of an animal.

curassow(KOOR • ah • soh) —a kind of turkey that lives in a jungle.

enemy(EN • ih • mee) —not a friend.

equator(ee • KWAI • ter) —the imaginary line that goes around the middle of the earth and divides the earth into the Northern and Southern hemisphere.

fern(FIRN) —a type of green plant that does not have flowers or seeds.

gecko(GECK • oh) —a lizard that has pads on its toes and can walk on walls and ceilings.

iguana(ih • GWAN • ah) —a large lizard that lives in hot, humid places.

island(EYE • land) —land surrounded on all sides by water.

jaguar(JAG • wahr) —a large, spotted wild cat that lives in hot, humid regions.

jungle(JUNG • il) —a region of the world that is hot and humid and has a thick growth of trees and other plants.

marvel(MAR • vil) —admire.

moss(MAWSS) —a type of small, green plant that does not have flowers.

orchid(OR • kid) —a plant that has unusual shaped flowers.

palm(PAHM) —a type of tree that grows in warm places.

peccary(PECK • ah • ree) —a wild pig.

periwinkle(PAIR • ee • wink • il) —a plant that can grow both small or large depending on where it is.

poison(POY • zun) —something that can cause sickness or death.

slender(SLEN • der) —thin; not wide.

sloth(SLAWTH) —an animal that lives in trees in hot, humid places and hangs upside down.

spear(SPEER) —a weapon with a sharp, pointed head.

spice(SPYSS) —material from a plant that smells and tastes strong or pleasant.

strangle(STRANG • il) —to squeeze or choke and kill something.

tamandua(tah • man • DWAH) —a kind of an anteater.

tapir(TAY • per) —an animal with a heavy body, short legs, and a long snout.

tropical(TROP • ih • kul) —a region where it is hot and humid.

tusk(TUHSSK) —a long, pointed tooth that sticks outside of an animal's mouth.

vine(VYNE) —a plant whose stem climbs on, creeps along, or twists around something else for support.

warlike(WOR • like) —quick to make war; not friendly.

INDEX

About the Author

Born and raised in western Iowa, Illa Podendorf has had experience teaching science at both elementary and high school levels. For many years she served as head of the Science Department, Laboratory School, University of Chicago and is currently consultant on the series of True Books and author of many of them. A pioneer in creative teaching, she has been especially successful in working with the gifted child.